The Museo Correr
in Venice

Cover
Vittore Carpaccio, *Two Venetian Noblewomen*. Sala 38.

Ala Napoleonica, seat
of the Museo Correr.

Translation
Richard Sadleir

Eugenia Bianchi
Nadia Righi
Maria Cristina Terzaghi

The Museo Correr in Venice

Electa

Museo Correr

The Ala Napoleonica of Piazza San Marco and the Procuratie Nuove are now the premises of the Museo Correr. This important collection illustrates the civic and cultural heritage of Venice; its name commemorates Teodoro Correr (1750–1830), who founded the collection. A dedicated collector, on his death this Venetian nobleman left thousands of objects and paintings which formed the core of the present holdings of the civic museums. The collection, first opened to the public in 1836, used to be housed in the Correr family's palace on the Grand Canal at San Zandegolà. Subsequent donations and acquisitions enlarged the collection until it had to be moved to the Fondaco dei Turchi, in a nearby palace specially fitted out as a museum and opened in 1887. The principle underlying the new layout was to document Venetian history and civilisation; so it was divided into sections, each dealing with an aspect of Venetian social life in the 16th and 17th centuries. This arrangement remains substantially unchanged today. In 1922 the museum moved to its present premises in the Procuratie Nuove, with access from the large staircase of the Ala Napoleonica on the piazza. Some sections of the civic museums have now been relocated to create collections which have premises of their own but are still part of the civic heritage. An example is Correr's collection of 18th-century paintings which, together with later acquisitions, have been on display since 1936 in the splendid setting of Ca' Rezzonico, while 19th-century paintings are held in the gallery of modern art in Ca' Pesaro. Since 1953 the Casa Goldoni in San Polo has housed a library, archives, and other facilities. It has recently been decided to bring together the rich collection of textiles in Ca' Mocenigo at San Stae to create a centre for studies in the history of Textiles and Costume. The idea of screening off the side of the piazza facing the Basilica of San Marco by building the Palazzo Reale arose under the French Kingdom of Italy (1807). There was a pressing need for a large building whose central features would be the Ballroom and a splendid staircase. The architect of the new building was Giuseppe Soli, but the design was altered, and it was only constructed in 1830–1840. The museum occupies most of the rooms of the ancient Palace and is divided into a number of sections. The fine Neo-Classical interiors of the first-floor make an ideal setting for the works of Antonio Canova. Three of these rooms have been open to the public since June 1996. The first floor also contains the historical section of the museum; particularly interesting is the section devoted to cartography, a science which reached remarkable heights at quite an early date in representations of Venice. There are rooms devoted to Crafts and Trades, Games and Festivals, with the aim of representing aspects of everyday life in the past, so reflecting the interests of the

Giovanni Bellini,
Dead Christ Supported
by Two Angels, *detail.*

museum's founder. The first floor also has a rich collection of bronzes (recently enlarged).

The second floor contains the splendid picture gallery, with important masterpieces of Venetian art from the origins down to the Renaissance; and there is a museum devoted to the Risorgimento period.

The present design of the installation is by the architect Carlo Scarpa, who worked on it in two periods, 1952–1953 and 1960, when the picture gallery was laid out. The Museo del Risorgimento was designed by the City of Venice's art department in 1980. The rooms devoted to Arts and Trades and Games date from 1993.

Between 1806 and 1814, under the Kingdom of Italy created by Napoleon, Venice was second only to Milan in importance and it therefore required a royal palace and public state rooms.

Eugène Beauharnais ordered a sumptuous staircase to be built on the site of the church of San Geminiano, a fine building by Jacopo Sansovino. The architects chosen were Giuseppe Soli and Lorenzo Santi. The present *Glory of Neptune* frescoed on the ceiling by

Piazza San Marco, View of the Procuratie Nuove and the Ala Napoleonica which now houses the Museo Correr.

Vogel-Richter, View of Piazza San Marco Towards the Ancient Church of San Geminiano, *engraving.*

Sebastiano Santi dates from 1837–1838, when the palace was largely restructured.

The staircase leads to the ante-room, with the ticket office, wardrobe and bookshop, and leads into the exhibition area.

Bernardino Castelli, Portrait of Teodoro Correr, *founder of the collection.*

Monumental staircase in the Palazzo Reale giving access to the museum.

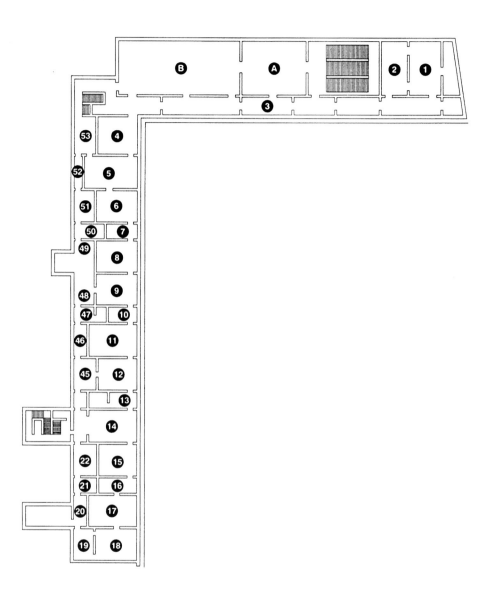

*Plan of the
Museo Correr*
First floor.
A. Antechamber-Ticket
    Office-Bookshop-
    Wardrobe
B Ballroom
1. Exhibition room
   and Cafeteria
2. Fine Arts room

3. Canova's Gallery
4. Throne Room
5. Dining Room
6–18.Venetian Civilization
19–22. Miniature Bronzes
45–53.Venetian Civilization

Room 1 and Room of the Fine Arts

The **first floor** is laid out in three large sections: Rooms 1–5 are devoted to Canova; 6–18 and 45–53 to Venetian life and culture; 19–22 to bronzes. **Room 1** is to the left of the visitor and decorated with floral motifs. Between the two windows is the Portrait of Teodoro Correr by Bernardino Castelli, known to have been painted before 1795, when an engraving was made from it. Further on is the **Room of the Fine Arts**, frescoed, like many other interiors of the palace, by Giuseppe Borsato. Figures, in perfect Empire style, are by Piero Moro. The spaces beyond are used for temporary exhibitions and at the far end is a coffee shop. The core of the rooms which are devoted to the celebrated Venetian sculptor Antonio Canova (Canova's Gallery, Throne Room, Dining Room and Ballroom) constituted the principal state rooms of the Palazzo Reale built from 1804 onwards and restructured in 1835-1840.

Pietro Moro and Giuseppe Borsato, wall decorations in the Fine Arts room.

Canova's Gallery

Entering the **Canova's Gallery** (also called the **Loggia Napoleonica**), which runs along the shorter side of Piazza San Marco opposite the basilica, one sees Canova's *Self-Portrait*, a plaster of Paris cast of the sculpture carved in 1812 and kept at Possagno.

Along the walls are numerous works cast in plaster of Paris and never carved in marble. They represent episodes from the Homeric poems and Plato's *Phaedo* (they date from some time between 1787 and 1792). Two represent *Works of Mercy*. On the left, as you enter, there is the *Death of Priam*, the mythical king of Troy, and to the right the *Dance of the Sons of Alcinous*; further on (right) are the *Trojans Offering the Peplum to Paris, Breiseis Consigned to the Heralds* and the *Return of Telemachus to Ithaca*. On the left the subjects

are *Feed the Hungry* and *Teach the Ignorant*. These last two reliefs (the second is signed and dated 1796) represent two of the seven Works of Mercy; they were probably commissioned by Senator Abbondio Rezzonico of Rome, to adorn a free school which the nobleman had founded near Bassano. The *Fruit Baskets*, dated 1774, displayed at the end of this part of the loggia, were carved for the balustrade of the palace of Daniele Farsetti at San

Lucas; they are thus among Canova's earliest works. Continuing along the gallery we come, on the right, to a preparatory study for the *Monument to Titian*, and on the left the *Herm* of the *Vestal Tuccia* and the *Herm* of *Sappho*. These last two works in plaster of Paris were given by Canova to the daughter of Doge Paolo Renier.

Room 3: the gallery closes with the fine cast of *Paris*, with carved on the trunk the date 12 May 1807. This cast, with the holes of the mould still visible, illustrates the process by which the marble statues were made from the cast. The *Paris* was donated to the museum by the Falier family, which had received it from Canova himself; two marble versions of it exist, one carved for Josephine Beauharnais (1807–1812) and the other for Louis of Bavaria (1810–1816).

Antonio Canova,
Feed the Hungry,
plaster bas-relief.

Antonio Canova ,
Death of Priam,
plaster bas-relief.

Antonio Canova,
Monument to Titian,
maquette.

Ballroom, Throne Room
and Dining Room

Next to Room 3 is the **Ballroom**. This splendid interior was designed by the architect Lorenzo Santi, beginning in 1822. Work and alterations went on for a long time, and it was only completed twenty years later, in 1843. The spacious rectangular chamber ends and is enhanced by the loggia for the orchestra, whose curved and gilded balustrades create the illusion that the room is actually oval. The decorations are by Giuseppe Borsato. This room contains the group of *Orpheus and Eurydice*, carved by Canova in Vicenza stone. It is an early work which was exhibited at the Fiera dell'Ascensione in 1777 and placed in the garden of Villa Falier at Asolo. The artist carved the figures at two different times, *Eurydice* being the earlier. Along the edge of the pedestal runs an inscription with verses of Virgil and Ovid alluding to the myth of Orpheus, who descended into Hades to recover his bride Eurydice, charming the terrible guardians of the underworld with his music. His wish was granted, provided he did not turn to look at her before they were safely above the ground;

Francesco Hayez,
Thetys Immerses
Achilles in the Waters
of Styx, *detached fresco.*
Throne Room.

Francesco Hayez,
Mercury Gives Paris
the Apple of Discord,
detached fresco.
Throne Room.

Antonio Canova,
Orpheus and Eurydice,
1777. Ballroom.

but overcome by desire he failed to keep the pact and she was lost to him.

At the end of the Ballroom there is an ante-chamber with bas-reliefs similar to those in the gallery. They represent three episodes from Plato's *Phaedo*: from left to right, *Socrates Leaves His Family*, *Socrates Drinks the Hemlock*, and *Criton Closes Socrates' Eyes*. On the left are displayed two *Virtues*: *Charity* and *Hope*.

Further on we come to what was once the **Throne Room (Room 4)**, decorated with frescoes by Giuseppe Borsato, while the lunettes with a gold ground are by Giovanni Battista Canal (c. 1811–1813). The frescoes on the walls have been removed and transferred to canvas. They were part of the original decoration of the palace. Those by Francesco Hayez (1817) are in the Sala del Generale Consiglio (Procuratie Nuove), while the charming *Four Seasons* by Giovanni Carlo Bevilacqua (1813) are still on the wall opposite the windows. Also by Bevilacqua is the allegorical fresco of *Victory Leading Faith to Crown Europe* (1814). Framed by stucco decorations, Hayez's paintings were removed in 1950. The monochrome medallions depict episodes from the *Iliad*: *Thetys Receives the Arms*

Antonio Canova,
Daedalus and Icarus,
1778–1779.
Throne Room.

of Achilles from Vulcan, and *Jove and Juno*; above the door are *Mercury Gives Paris the Apple of Discord*, and *Thetys Immerses Achilles in the Waters of Styx*. Below the monochrome medallions are compartments with elegant *Dancers*. Between the windows is the cast of *Winged Cupid* which Canova carved for the Russian Prince Yusupov in 1793–1797. At the centre of the room stands the splendid group of *Daedalus and Icarus* from the Palazzo Pisani in Venice.

Room 5 was formerly the dining-room of the palace and is one of its best-preserved Neo-Classical interiors. The rich decoration is by Giuseppe Borsato. Particularly noteworthy are the charming *Views* set in the tondos between the wall decorations. Venice, in the tondo on the left of the entrance, is represented by Piazza San Marco during a flood. These landscapes gave the room one of its names, *Sala dei Paesaggi*. The ceiling fresco by Giovanni Carlo Bevilacqua depicts *Olympus*. On the easel are two paintings by Canova: on the right, the uncompleted *Portrait of Amadeo Svajer* and to the left is *Cupid and Psyche*. The Neo-Classical table in the centre of the room is a very fine piece: the top in white and blue Sèvres porcelain is decorated with mythological

and allegorical scenes. A similar table, once owned by Josephine Beauharnais, is at Malmaison. Between the windows is a plaster of Paris cast of the *Italian Venus*.

Daedalus and Icarus were commissioned by the Procurator Pietro Vettor Pisani, whose daughters later donated it to the city of Venice. It is a youthful work. The two protagonists of the tragic myth related by Ovid are delicately depicted at one of the most melancholy moments: when the aged Daedalus applies the waxen wings to the shoulders of Icarus, unmindful of his tragic end. Seized by enthusiasm for flight, the youth soars too near the sun, which melts the waxen wings. At the feet of the figures Canova represented the tools used to carve marble, a detail justified by Daedalus's craft, but also an allusion to Sculpture, of which this statue is such a splendid allegory.

Antonio Canova, Portrait of the Celebrated Antiquary Amedeo Svajer. *Dining Room.*

Rooms 6–7

Room 6 begins the display of objects illustrating Venetian life and culture. The theme of this and the next room is the figure of the **doge**, the highest office of the Venetian magistracy. Of remote origins, the powers of the holder of this office changed through the centuries; but he had always to be of patrician rank and his appointment was for life. Of great interest in this first room are the two paintings on the wall to the right of the entrance, originally organ doors from the church of San Michele in Isola. Painted by the Brescian artists Giovanni and Bernardino da Asola in 1526, they represent (left) *St. Benedict and Two Monks* and (right) *Doge Pietro Orseolo Before St. Romualdo*. Pietro Orseolo abandoned the dogeship to become a Benedictine monk in an abbey in the Pyrenees, where he died in 987. On the wall by the entrance hangs the great canvas of Aliense (Antonio Vassilacchi) depicting the *Arrival of Queen Caterina Cornaro of Cyprus* which took place in 1489. The painting is from the Doge's Palace. Opposite is a painting by Andrea Michiel, in the same format, of the *Arrival of the Dogaressa Morosina Morosini Grimani at the Doge's Palace*, an event that took place in 1597. Another poetic episode in the life of the doges is recounted in the painting between the windows by Gian Antonio Guardi; it is a replica of the painting by Paris Bordone for the Scuola Grande di San Marco (now in the Gallerie dell'Accademia). This is the *Presentation of the Ring to the Doge*: a fisherman gives the doge the ring received from St. Mark. Note the very fine *Portrait of Francesco Foscari* by Lazzaro Bastiani (c. 1460): the doge and *condottiero* is represented with all the honours of his office. The display cases contain precious objects also associated with the office. Of particular note is the fragment of a tapestry displayed between the showcases, with its outstanding *Portrait of Doge Lorenzo Grimani* (or Leonardo Loredan), part of the altarpiece that was traditionally presented to the basilica of San Marco after the doge took the oath of office. **Room 7** is devoted more specifically to the solemn moment of the **doge's election** and the civic festivities he presided over. The electoral system was highly complicated so as to avoid irregularities, as is shown by the objects in the display cabinet on the right. On the left wall is a woodcut by Matteo Pagan (1559), illustrating one of the most significant public events in the doge's life: the *Doge's Procession to Piazza San Marco*. The painting by Heintz on the left wall illustrates the *Procession for the Feast of the Redeemer*: the doge would go every year with a procession of boats to the church of the Redentore to give thanks for the end of the terrible plague of 1576.

Lazzaro Bastiani,
Portrait of Doge
Francesco Foscari.
Sala del Doge.

Portrait of Doge Lorenzo
Grimani (or Leonardo
Loredan), *fragment
of a tapestry.*
Sala del Doge.

Matteo Pagano,
Doge's Procession
in Piazza San Marco,
engraving, detail.
*Sala dell'elezione
del Doge.*

Room 8

The very fine **bookcases** in **Room 8** are from the convent of San Nicola da Tolentino, of the Theatine Order, which was suppressed in the Napoleonic period. The furnishings were then moved to Palazzo Pisani. They include 17th century inlaid furniture in solid walnut which contain manuscripts and fine books from the 16th and 17th centuries and the doge's Commissions which are a feature of the museum. The showcases at the centre of the room contain books with fine silver and leather bindings. The 18th-century chandelier is particularly beautiful; like that in the following chamber it was produced by the Murano glassworks of Giuseppe Briati. After the doge, the major officers in the Venetian magistracy were the senators and procurators. The latter supervised and administered the Basilica of San Marco, and gave their name to the range of buildings—the Procuratie—facing the square, where they used to meet.

Teatini Library.
The 18th-century chandelier
was produced by Giuseppe
Briati's workshop
on Murano.

Rooms 9–12

Room 9 and **Room 10** (**Sale delle Magistrature**) are the portraits of some of these magistrates, originally in Palazzo Morosini. The Procurators can be recognised by the velvet stole covering their shoulders. In **Room 10** there is a very fine *Portrait of Vincenzo Querini* by the painter Bartolomeo Nazari of Bergamo (18th century). Over the door of the previous chamber, there is the equally interesting *Portrait of Pietro Balbi*, from the Cinquecento Veneto school.

The museum's rich collection of medals is partly displayed in cabinets in **Room 11** (**Numismatics**). Of great interest is the complete series of coins struck by the Venetian Republic. A curiosity is the collection of "Oselle" in the cabinet on the right. These were gold and silver medals, often current coin, which were issued to commemorate the gift of birds made by the doge every New Year to the Venetian patricians. The finances of the state were under the charge of three functionaries called "Camerlenghi." We see them depicted in the fine canvas by Jacopo Tintoretto (on the wall by the entrance to the room): the subject of the painting is

Batolomeo Nazari,
Portrait of Doge Vincenzo
Querini.
Sala delle Magistrature.

St. Justine in the act of protecting these three functionaries, identified as Marco Giustiniani, Angelo Morosini and Alessandro Badoer. The painting was originally in the Palazzo dei Camerlenghi on Rialto. On the left-hand wall hangs an enormous naval ensign with the arms of Doge Domenico Contarini.

The sea was all-important in the history of Venice. The city's fleet, the instrument of defence and dominion, was the source of its political and commercial power. In the middle of **Room 12 (Venice and the sea)** can be seen two models of galleys, the swift craft designed for war and the defence of the lagoon, and also for the escort of merchant ships. A collection of the very fine lamps hung on the galleys are also displayed at the centre of the room. The cabinets contain instruments of navigation. On the end wall hang two canvases by an anonymous 16th century Venetian painter depicting episodes from the battle of Lepanto (1571), where Venice defeated the Turks. The side walls have 17th-century paintings showing the battle array of the Turkish and Venetian fleets.

16th century Veneto school, Battle of Lepanto, *room dedicated to Venice and the sea.*

Jacopo Tintoretto, St. Justine and the Treasurers. *Room devoted to Numismatics.*

Antonio di Natale, Plan of the Arsenal, *water-colour. Sala dell'Arsenal.*

Rooms 13–14

Room 13 is devoted to the **Arsenal**, the shipyards where the naval fleet and, in some cases, merchant ships were fitted out. Very rare and of the greatest interest is the 18th-century water-colour of the *Plan of the Arsenal* by Antonio di Natale (left wall); it was unusual for the Arsenal to be painted because of the secrecy shrouding the construction of warships. Also noteworthy is the *Portrait of Angelo Memmo IV in the Uniform of Admiral of the Fleet* by Alessandro Longhi. It depicts clearly the red damask with gold brocade of the costume worn by the commander of the fleet. Quite accurate depictions of the city of Venice are common from early times. The

collection of plans in **Room 14 (Venezia Forma Urbis)** are thus of great interest, starting from the celebrated 16th-century engraving of the plan of Venice by Jacopo de Barbari; the gigantic plate from which it was taken is also displayed. On the wall opposite are hung paintings that illustrate the changes to the 16th-century plan through the centuries: there is a late 16th- or early-17th-century canvas by Giovan Battista Arzenti and a mid-17th-century view in perspective by Giovan Battista Heintz. On the end wall hangs the symbol of Venice, the Lion of St. Mark, a 17th century wooden sculpture from the chancel of the basilica of San Marco. Opposite is the plaque

known as the *Edict of Egnazio*: it was carved by the humanist Giovan Battista Cipelli and comes from the headquarters of the Magistrato alle Acque, which supervised the security of the waters of the lagoon; it is a solemn admonition to whoever might threaten the peace of the Republic by sea. The central space is occupied by two large globes by the Venetian cartographer Vincenzo Coronelli (1650–1718): they represent the celestial globe and the earth.

Rooms 15–18

Next follow **Room 15** and **Room 16 (Correr Armoury)**. They are devoted to Venice's military power. The weapons on display, Italian and European, come from the collection by Teodoro Correr. Room 15 contains armour from the 15th and 16th centuries. Note (first on the left) the ship-armour with Nuremberg punch-work. The fire-arms and cutting weapons date from the 14th, 15th and 17th centuries. On the end wall hangs a Turkish fabric with an inscription from the Koran in Arabic script. The next room contains fire-arms, including a ship's cannon with twelve mouths, called an "Organo" (17th century). Also interesting are some of the pistols in the display cases, including one from a Brescian workshop, bearing the maker's name, LAZARINO COMINAZO, on the barrel (c. 1670).
The museum has a wealth of items related to the exploits of Francesco Morosini, the celebrated condottiero nicknamed "il Peleponnesiaco" or conqueror of the Peleponnese. They were acquired in 1895 and transferred to the Civic Collections from the palace of the Morosini family at Santo Stefano; now they are partly collected in **Room 17** (Sala Morosini). Morosini won a number of victories against the Turks and was also celebrated for his conquest of Athens (during which he destroyed the Parthenon). Elected doge in 1688, he died in battle in 1694 during one of his campaigns against the Turks. On the right of the room as one enters there are cannons of various sizes, for use on galleys, and 17th-century harquebuses. The arms of the family, carved in wood, hang from the wall. On the left of the entrance is a set of six paintings of the 17th century Venetian school which illustrate episodes in Morosini's life. Between the windows is the imposing triple ship's lamp that hung on the poop of Morosini's galley in his last campaign against the Turks. Other objects belonging to the doge are on display, including a prayer-book and prie-dieu from his flagship. Also note two paintings by Gregorio Lazzarini, replicas of those on the Arco Morosini in the Doge's Palace celebrating the condottiero.
Room 18 (Morosini Armoury) contains trophies and plunder won by Francesco Morosini. On the wall hangs a Portrait of the Doge on Horseback by Giovanni Carboncino dating from 1688, the year of his election. The cabinets contain 17th century Oriental (right) and Venetian weapons (left).The shields on the walls are part of the Morosini war booty taken from the Turks.

17th century Veneto school, Portrait of Doge Francesco Morosini. *Sala Morosini.*

View of the Correr Armoury.

Alessandro Piazza, Francesco Morosini Leaving St. Mark's Basin for the Levant. *Sala Morosini.*

Rooms 19–22

Rooms 19-20-21-22 display part of the museum's rich collection of **miniature bronzes**. Bronzes were a form of art that had their heyday in the Renaissance; Cinquecento bronzes of this kind are mostly copies of celebrated masterpieces of Classical art on a reduced scale and hence easy to handle. They were so popular that they became an independent form of art and often reached surprising artistic heights. In Northern Italy, Padua and Venice were especially renowned for their bronzes.

In Venice two illustrious sculptors, Tullio and Antonio Lombardo, were outstanding in this field.

In **Room 19** the cabinet against the left-hand wall contains examples of their work. Note the *Venus with a Diadem* and the *Bust of a Woman*. Padua, with the spectacular altar by Donatello in the Basilica of Sant'Antonio and a proud antiquarian tradition, was inevitably a leader in popularising this art form and raising it to levels of great refinement. It was, in fact, a pupil of Donatello, Bartolomeo Bellano, who commenced production of

such bronzes in Padua. But it was above all Andrea Briosco, known as Riccio (1470/75–1532), who was the supreme master of the art and created a flourishing workshop. He also revealed the practical qualities of such bronzes, which could be adapted to the most varied domestic uses—ink-pots, lamp-

Workshop of Severo da Ravenna (attributed to), David with the Head of Goliath. *Room 19.*

holders, etc. His objects also intrigue by their naturalism, which combines myth and fantasy and makes them very differ-ent from his other, more monumental and classical sculptures. These bronzes diverge widely from the dictates of Reniassance art, with its emphasis on an Apollonian classicism, and seem to draw on the Dionysian and popular spirit which also pervades primitive mediaeval sculpture. Miniature bronzes from the workshops of Riccio and Severo da Ravenna are displayed in the cabinets in Room 19. **Room 20** is devoted to **Utensils**, in which the workshops of Alberghetti and that of Giuseppe di Levi from Verona dominated the Venetian market. They include bells with handles of various forms, ink-pots and mortars. The next room **(Room 21)** exhibits the work of two great 16th-century architects and sculptors: Jacopo Sansovino and Alessandro Vittoria. Sansovino came to Venice from Florence, where he had made his name as a sculptor, and influenced the leading sculptor of the Venetian Cinquecento, Alessandro Vittoria (1552–1608). These display cases contain splendid bronzes, pervaded by an intense dynamism which foreshadows the Baroque and is very evident in the door-knockers; note that of *Neptune and Sea-Horses* in the central cabinet. **Room 22** has some fine items from the two great Venetian workshops active in the late 16th and early 17th centuries: the *bottega* of Tiziano Aspetti (1556–1607) and Niccolò Roccatagliata (active c. 1539–1636) produced the very fine *Bacchus Pouring Wine* in the central case; from that of Gerolamo Campagna (died 1626) comes the set of angels from the Venetian church of San Lorenzo, dating from 1615–1618.

From Room 22 we can take the staircase that leads to the Pinacoteca (Art Gallery) and the Museo Risorgimentale on the second floor; or else continue the tour of the rooms devoted to Venetian life and culture on the first floor.

Gerolamo Campagna, Salt-cellar in the form of Neptune holding a sea-shell. Room 20.

Alessandro Vittoria, doorknocker with Neptune and sea-horses. Room 21.

Paduan workshop (?), early 16th century, Boy Taking a Thorn from His Foot. *Room 19.*

Rooms 45–53

Room 45 focuses on the **Bucintoro**, the splendid state barge on board of which the doges celebrated the ritual betrothal with the sea. Each year on the Feast of the Ascension, the state barge was sailed to the Lido for the traditional rite. Already in use in the 14th century, the Bucintoro seems to have even more ancient origins. The last of these barges was built in 1722–1728, carved and gilded by Antonio Corradini. All that remains of it is the splendid hatch cover here on display, depicting *St. Mark*, the city's patron saint. Through this aperture the doge would cast the ring that wedded Venice to the sea.

Room 46 (Festivals). Festivals were the high points of the relationship between the city and its citizens. The three paintings by the 17th-century artist Heintz the Younger depict three of the many traditional festivities in the Venetian calendar: the *Entrance of the Patriarch Federico Corner to San Pietro di Castello*, with boats adorned for Carnival, the *Bull Chase in Campo San Paolo*, presented for the doge by the company of Becheri (butchers), and the *Boat Trip to Murano*.

Room 47 is a small room with three important paintings, including the *Family Portrait* attributed to Cesare Vecellio. **Rooms 48–51** are devoted to **Arts and Trades**. Venice was not, of course, the only city to have trade guilds in which all citizens and foreigners who practised the same calling were invited to enrol. In Venice each of these "Arti" had its own rules, known as *mariegole*. All the Venetian guilds came under the "Magistratura della Giustizia Vecchia," with its headquarters in the Palazzo dei Camerlenghi. The signs of the guilds in this room come from this palace and were probably used to display notices about the guilds' rules, fees and guild activities. In the 16th and 17th centuries they were made of wood, with the arms of the Magistratura della Giustizia Vecchia, the lion of St. Mark and the guild's patron saint, to whom an altar would be dedicated in one of the churches. **Room 50** is wholly devoted to the **Arte dei Dipintori** (painters' guild),

and contains the artistic 18th-century sign with *St. Lucy*, while **Room 51** is devoted to the **Arte dei Tagliapietra** (masons). Another interesting chapter of Venetian life was the city's **games**, documented in **Rooms 52–53**: they bring out, among other things, a rather cynical and disenchanted side of Venice. Gambling became socially acceptable as early as the start of the 17th century, with special premises established for it in 1638: the foyer of Palazzo Dandolo at San Moisè. This was the city's first public *casino*. The pictures in Room 52 illustrate the *Forze d'Ercole*, acrobatic displays popular at festivities.

18th century Veneto school, Sign of a Guild. Sala delle Arti e dei Mestieri.

Antonio Corradini, Hatch-cover of the Doge's barge. Sala del Bucintoro.

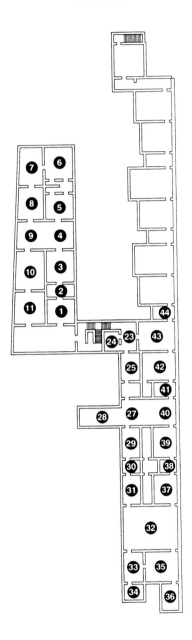

Second Floor

The staircase by Room 22 leads to the **Second Floor**: on the right is the **Picture Gallery**, on the left the **Museo Risorgimentale**.

With his passion for history, Teodoro Correr clearly understood the documentary value of paintings.

During the years of the late 18th and early 19th century few collectors bothered with the 15th century; so the noble Venetian, though his contemporaries looked at him askance, was able to easily acquire Quattrocento Venetian paintings of remarkable beauty (above all by Giovanni Bellini, Antonello da Messina and Cosmè Tura) and numerous paintings by Pietro Longhi, an 18th century Venetian painter, so completely ignoring market tendencies.

The 18th-century works have been placed in Ca' Rezzonico, while paintings from the primitives to the early 16th century have been installed on the second floor of the Procuratie Nuove; the Museo Correr has one of the largest and most select collections of the latter in the world.

Early Venetian painting has close links with the art of the nearby Eastern Empire, of which Venice formed one boundary and also a link with the West.

Down to the first half of the 13th century, mosaic cycles were one of the most outstanding features of Venetian art. The Basilica of San Marco is a remarkable showcase of these.

The artists who worked in the basilica either came from Byzantium or were generally under the influence of its hieratic art, as also happened in many other Italian towns at that time, including Rome.

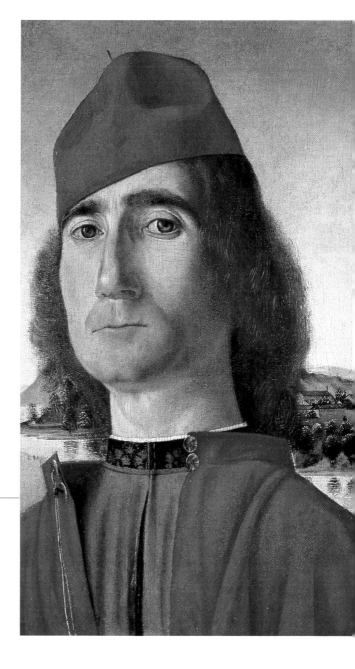

Ferrarese/Bolognese painter c. 1490–95, Man with a Red Beret.

Room 24

Room 24 (Veneto-Byzantine painters) contains works in the courtly and refined style of the second half of the 13th century and first half of the 14th.

It was only in about the 1260s that the first frescoes or panel paintings appeared in Venice; previously mosaic was dominant.

In particular, note one of the earliest examples of Venetian panel painting: the sepulchral casket known as the *Cassa "della beata Giuliana" di Collalto*, who died in 1262. It comes from the monastery of Santi Biagio e Cataldo at the Giudecca; its name derives from the depiction, inside the lid, of the Blessed Juliana kneeling before the saints to whom the monastery was dedicated. The painter's Western expressiveness—and rejection of the schemes of Byzantine art—are particularly marked.

Veneto painter from the mid-13th century, Chest of the Blessed Juliana.

Veneto-Byzantine painter active in the mid-14th century, Crucifixion with Saints.

Room 25

The glass door leads to **Room 25**, devoted to **Paolo Veneziano and Venetian painters of the 14th century**. Known to have been active between 1333 and 1358 and to have died before September 1362, Paolo is one of the key figures in the emancipation of Venetian painting from Byzantine models. Yet his stylistic development is the reverse of what one might expect. Paolo's earliest work seems more deeply personal and closer to mainland traditions, while the later work is more obedient to the dictates of Eastern art. The paintings in this room date from his later period: the *Six Saints* (Augustine, Peter, John the Baptist, John the Evangelist, Paul and George) is from a polyptych (the central panel is lost) from the parish church of Grisolera, and the very fine *St. John the Baptist*. This is probably a fragment from the Venetian cathedral of San Pietro in Castello, and is a good example of the combination of refined Eastern tradition with Western Gothic. The other 14th-century polyptyches in this room exemplify aspects of Venetian painting in the period: the triptych with folding panels on the left

represents the *Crucifixion, Stories of Christ and the Virgin, Allegorical and Mystical Figures, Prophets and Fathers of the Church*, a "summa" of the figurative repertoire of the period. The two paintings of the *Madonna and Child* and the triptych

with the *Madonna, Pietà* and *Saints* reveal clearly the relationship between art in the Veneto and Greek Dalmatian and Cretan painting. Also of interest is the painting of *St. Peter*, attributed to a painter from the Veneto in the mid-14th century.

Paolo Veneziano,
St. John the Baptist,
fragment of a panel.

Room 26

The work of **Lorenzo Veneziano (Room 26)** is documented in Venice between 1356 and 1372. His paintings, unlike Paolo's, are firmly in the mainstream of Gothic art then triumphant in the Po valley. There are two fine works of his here: on the left is part of a larger polyptych with *Figures and Stories of Saints* and on the right another panel of a polyptych signed and dated 1369 along one edge; it represents the *Giving of the Keys to St. Peter*: the remaining fragments of this work are in Berlin. The *Four Saints* at the far end of the room, long attributed to Lorenzo, is probably by a follower of his, Jacobello Bonomo (documented between 1370–1390).

Lorenzo Veneziano, polyptych with Figures and Stories of Saints.

Room 27

The lacy stonework of the reliefs on certain Venetian palaces mostly date from the period of **Decorated Gothic (Room 27)**, a style that originated in the North of Europe and had a long history in Venice. The reliefs in Room 27 are from this period. Worthy of note is the statue carved by one of the great masters of the period, Iacobello Dalle Masegne (who also carved the Iconostasis in San Marco): this represents the Doge Antonio Venier kneeling; originally he would also have been holding a standard. Instead of following established official models, the statue is charged with dramatic tension and seems to be a true portrait.

Also of great interest are the fragments of fresco removed from a private house near San Marco and transferred to canvas (on the right-hand and end walls).

Veneto painter of the 14th century, Allegory of the Virtues, *detail of a detached fresco.*

Iacobello Dalle Masegne, Portrait of Doge Antonio Venier Kneeling, *marble.*

Room 28

Room 28 is devoted to **Gothic painting** and arranged in two sections. The first part (Room 28.1) contains works from the late 14th century and early decades of the 15th; the second (Room 28.2) displays paintings by one of the leading 14th-century artists in Venice: Stefano Veneziano, or Stefano di Sant'Agnese, as well as other artists active at the end of the century. The works in the first section include the *Madonna with Child, St. Paul and St. John the Baptist*, recently attributed to a painter of Rimini known as the Maestro dell'Arengo, and a *Crucifix* painted on both sides so that the images could always be visible to the faithful when it was carried in procession. Stefano Veneziano painted the fine *Madonna and Child Enthroned* (first on the left), a work signed dated 1369, and the later *St. Christopher with the Christ Child*, parts of a single polyptych painted for the Scuola dei Forneri at the Madonna dell'Orto, now in the church of San Zaccaria, dated 1385. There is also a *St. Michael* from the bottega of a Paduan master of the period of Guariento, and *Four Saints*, attributed to Jacobello di Bonomo.

Stefano di Sant'Agnese,
Madonna and Child.

Workshop of Guariento,
The Archangel Michael.

Room 29

The next room, **Room 29,** is divided into two sections: Room 29.1 (**International Gothic: the origins**) and 29.2 (**International Gothic: the protagonists**). They contain masterpieces of the refined Gothic art that spread through the courts of all Europe from the end of the 14th century and all through the 15th. Various cities of the Veneto (especially Venice and Padua) were leading centres of this style. Among the pioneers in the first section are the *Madonna and Child in a Garden,* ascribed to a painter active in Verona in the first half of the Quattrocento, and, the fine panel painted on both sides, with *Angelic Musicians* on the front and *St. Cosma* on the back, probably by a Venetian painter, largely influenced by Michelino da Besozzo, another leading representative of International Gothic. These are probably the doors of the predella of a polyptych which has been dismembered. Also note the two interesting panels with the *Martyrdom* and *Death of St. Mamete* by Francesco de' Franceschi, a Venetian painter who was active in the mid–15th century and influenced by Antonio Vivarini's style. The second section of this room contains works by two of the major International Gothic artists in Venice: Jacobello del Fiore and Michele Giambino. Jacobello (documented from 1400–1439) was responsible for the very tender *Madonna and Child* bearing the artist's signature and dating from 1420–1430.

The refined elegance of Michele Giambino is evident in the *Madonna and Child with a Goldfinch.* The room also has other paintings by Tuscan masters of this style: the *St. Ermagora and St. Fortunato* by Matteo Giovannetti, an assistant of Simone Martini, and fragments of some chests painted by the anonymous Master of the Jarves chests, decorated with *Stories of Alatiel.*

Jacobello del Fiore,
Madonna and Child.

*Follower of Michelino
da Besozzo,* Choir of
Angels.

*Francesco de'
Franceschi,* Martyrdom
of St. Mamete.

*Master of the Jarves
chest*, Stories of Alatiel.
*Sala dei Protagonisti del
Gotico Internazionale.*

Room 30

The *Pietà* by the Ferrarese artist **Cosmè Tura** in **Room 30** clearly reveals Teodoro Correr's intelligence as a collector: this work was completely out of favour in the period when it was acquired but it is of fundamental importance in understanding the influences at work on 15th-century painting in the Veneto. It is an original combination of Northern European qualities with motifs from the paintings of Piero della Francesca and the sculptures of Donatello: it can be dated to about 1468. The room also contains a small *Portrait of a Man* attributed to a painter notably influenced by the school of Ferrara.

Cosmè Tura, Pietà, *dating from c. 1468.*

Room 31

The room is divided into two sections. The first , **Room 31.1** contains Quattrocento works clearly of Ferrarese origin. Note especially the *Madonna and Child* formerly attributed to Francesco Benaglio, dating from the end of the 15th century. The Madonna clearly reveals the relationship with Central Italian painters, notably Piero della Francesca, an influence widely felt in the art of Ferrara.

The second section, **Room 31.2**, is devoted to the painter Bartolomeo Vivarini of Murano and his pupil Leonardo Boldrini. After training in Padua, Vivarini came under the influence of Andrea Mantegna. On display are two versions of the *Madonna and Child*: the one on the right is signed and can be dated to about 1460.

A peculiarity of these two works is the presence at this rather late date of the somewhat old-fashioned gold ground. Leonardo Boldrini, a Venetian and follower of Vivarini, is thought to have painted the *Nativity* and the *Presentation at the Temple* (c. 1475) and the later altar triptych with the *Madonna and Child*, *St. Jerome and St. Augustine*.

Francesco Benaglio,
Madonna and Child.

Leonardo Boldrini,
Nativity.

Room 32

Room 32 (Sala delle Quattro Porte) is one of the few chambers in the Procuratie Nuove to retain its original architecture (late 16th–early 17th century). The doorways, now walled up, are 18th-century work. The furnishings go back partly to the 16th and partly the 17th centuries. Apart from the fine woodwork, still well-preserved, note the papier-mâché *Madonna and Child* by Jacopo Sansovino. This late Cinquecento relief used to be in the Corte Scotti in Campo San Luca.

Bartolomeo Vivarini, Madonna and Child. *Sala delle Quattro Porte.*

Jacopo Sansovino, Madonna and Child, *papier-mâché. Sala delle Quattro Porte.*

Room 33

The active cultural links between Venice and the Flemish painters are partly illustrated by the next room, **Room 33 (Flemish painters of the 15th century)**. It contains interesting works like the *Adoration of the Magi* by Pieter Bruegel the Younger and *Christ in Limbo* by a follower of Hieronymus Bosch. Particularly refined are the panels painted on both sides with the *Annunciation* and *Two Saints*.

Pieter Bruegel
the Younger,
Adoration of the Magi.

Room 34

One of the greatest of all painters is **Antonello da Messina**, known to have been active in Venice in 1475–1476. He is represented in **Room 34** by a masterpiece, the *Pietà with Three Angels*, one of the museum's outstanding acquisitions. The painting is all the more precious as being Antonello's only work still in Venice, where his influence on the artistic tradition was profound. (Among other things, he probably introduced the technique of oil painting, hitherto used only by Flemish artists.) The panel was originally in the Doge's Palace, in the Sala del Consiglio dei Dieci, where Marco Boschini saw it and left a description in the 17th century. The painting is poorly preserved and seems to have lost the lower section; yet its quality is clearly apparent in the best-preserved sections, the landscape and the body of Jesus. It is unusual in that, though it was definitely painted in Venice, it depicts the church of San Francesco in Messina, a tribute by the painter to his native town. The room also has two splendid Flemish works: a *Crucifixion* by **Hugo van der Goes** and a *Madonna and Child* by **Dieric Bouts**, which both reflect the bonds between Antonello da Messina's art and that of Flanders.

Dieric Bouts, Madonna and Child.

Antonello da Messina,
Pietà with Three Angels,
the only work by the
Sicilian painter left
in Venice. Room 34.

Room 35

Room 35 (Flemish and German artists of the 15th and 16th centuries) brings together Flemish and German paintings, obviously much in demand in Venice, dating from the late 15th and early 16th centuries. Note the *Pleasures of the Prodigal Son*, by a painter in the circle of Paul Coecke , and the *Temptations of St. Antony*, by an artist influenced by Bosch, perhaps Herri Met de Bles, nicknamed "Civetta." There is also a *Portrait of* a Lady attributed to Bartholomeus Bruyn (1493–1555).

Circle of Paul Coecke, Pleasures of the Prodigal Son.

Follower of Bosch in Antwerp, The Temptations of St. Antony.

Room 36

Room 36 is one of the most significant in the museum and represents one of the peaks of Venetian painting. It contains works from the foremost Quattrocento painter's workshop in Venice, that of the **Bellini** family. Giovanni Bellini, like Antonello, was one of the greatest of Western painters. Teodoro Correr himself possessed three of his finest works: a *Crucifixion*, *The Dead Christ Supported by Two Angels* and a *Transfiguration*. The *Madonna and Child*, here displayed on an easel and commonly known as the Madonna Frizzoni, was donated to the museum in 1919

by Frizzoni, its last owner. These four remarkable paintings belong to Bellini's early period; the *Crucifixion*, probably done in about 1455 is actually one of his very

earliest works and was strongly influenced by his brother-in-law Andrea Mantegna. Jacopo, Giovanni's father, is here represented by a *Crucifixion*, which is part of the predella of which three other panels are in museums in Ferrara and Padua. It may have come from San Zaccaria. This is a work of great expressive power, probably painted in the mid-15th century, at the peak of his career. Gentile Bellini, Giovanni's brother, painted the noteworthy *Portrait of Doge Giovanni Mocenigo*, probably unfinished because of the painter's departure for Constantinople in 1475.

Gentile Bellini,
Portrait of
Doge Giovanni Mocenigo.

Jacopo Bellini,
Crucifixion.

Giovanni Bellini, The
Dead Christ Supported
by Two Angels.

Following pages
Giovanni Bellini,
Transfiguration.

Giovanni Bellini,
Crucifixion.

MISEREMINI·MEI·SALTEM
VOS·AMICI·MEI·

Room 37

Room 37 (Alvise Vivarini and minor artists of the late Quattrocento). Among painters active in the Veneto in the second half of the 14th century, this room exhibits the work of Alvise Vivarini, the heir to a great Muranese workshop, from which comes the *St. Antony* displayed on an easel (the frame is probably original). A *Sacra Conversazione* by Giovanni da Martino da Udine is dated 1498. A work of great beauty, despite its poor state of preservation, is the *Madonna and Child with St. Nicholas and St. Lawrence*, a mature work of Gian Battista Cima da Conegliano dating from the second decade of the16th century. Marco Basaiti may be the author of the fine *Portrait of a Man in a Cap* and Bartolomeo Montagna from Brescia, who painted the *Madonna and Child with St. Joseph*, dating from the early Cinquecento, were both influenced by Alvise Vivarini.

Marco Basaiti,
Portrait of Man in a Cap.

Marco Basaiti, Madonna and Child with Donor.

Bartolomeo Mantegna, Madonna and Child with St. Joseph.

Benedetto Diana, Pietà.

Room 38

Vittore Carpaccio
(c. 1460–1525/26) was one
of the most refined Venetian
painters of the later
Quattrocento. His art
embodies the splendour of
Venetian society in his day and
the Museo Correr has one of
his most celebrated paintings,
Two Venetian Noblewomen,
better known as *The
Courtesans*, the title given
it by Romantic literature
(**Room 38**). This panel, a
fragment of a larger
composition, can be dated
to the first decade of the
Cinquecento and is a work
of the artist's maturity. The
vase on the right side of
the painting bears the arms
of the Priuli family, to which
the women evidently belonged.
Also displayed here is *St. Peter
Martyr*, another late work,
part of a lost polyptych
originally in the Venetian
church of Santa Fosca.

**Two Venetian
Noblewomen**:
noblewomen or
unscrupulous courtesans?
The subject of this
celebrated work by
Carpaccio was much
debated until the recent
identification of a panel
at the Paul Getty

Museum, Malibu, as its
missing upper section. It
depicts a *Hunting Scene*
and sheds light on the
painting's true meaning:
two noblewomen, bored
and wearied, await their
husbands who are intent
on hunting waterfowl on
the lagoon. This

interpretation is
confirmed by many
symbolic details, such as
the women's dresses and
the objects in the
painting, as well as the
arms of the noble Priuli
family on the vase at the
right.

Vittore Carpaccio, Two
Venetian Noblewomen.

Room 39

In 1504 Carpaccio painted the cycle of *Stories of the Virgin* for the Scuola degli Albanesi. One of five paintings depicting the *Visitation* is in **Room 39 (Carpaccio and minor painters of the early Cinquecento)** together with other interesting 16th century Venetian works. A remarkably fine work is the *Portrait of a Gentleman in a Red Cap* (on an easel), by an unknown artist: he seems to have been from Ferrara or Bologna and active at the end of the Quattrocento. Also by an unknown master, but closer to the manner of Bellini, is the *Portrait of a Young Man in a Fur Coat* (also displayed on an easel). Though poorly preserved, the *Circumcision* by Marco Marziale is another admirable work. Also note the *Madonna and Child with St. Peter*, attributed to an artist close to Bissolo.

Marco Marziale,
The Circumcision.

Venetian painter
of the late 15th century,
Portrait of a Young Man
in a Fur Coat.

Room 40–44

The work of Lorenzo Lotto is remarkable in its development. He was an outstanding Venetian artist, mainly active in other parts of Italy. **Room 40 (Lorenzo Lotto and the High Renaissance. Collection of Ivories)** contains a *Madonna and Child* (displayed on an easel) painted in about 1525. Other paintings displayed are by Girolamo and Francesco da Santacroce, who trained in the shadow of Giovanni Bellini. Girolamo is the author of the *Nativity*, while Francesco did the *Vision of St. Jerome* as well as the *Madonna and Child, The Infant St. John the Baptist and Two Angels*. The display-cases contain French and German ivories of the 16th and 17th centuries. **Room 41** contains the work of **Greek Ikon-Painters from the 16th and 17th centuries.** Greek painters, mainly from Crete, were known as *Madonneri*, since their many Venetian workshops mainly turned out ikons for the popular market. The great Doménikos Theotokópoulos (called El Greco) was trained in this school. Two of the paintings here have been compared to his early work; they are the *Last Supper* and *St. Augustine at Prayer*.

The Civic Collections have a rich collection of **majolica**, only part of which is on display in **Room 42**, which contains a selection from the main 16th- and 17th-century schools. The **Manin Library** in **Room 43** comes from the palace of Ludovico Manin, the last of the doges, at San Salvador. The bookcases are late-18th century work, carved in the incipient Neo-Classical style. **Room 44 (Servizio Ridolfi)** contains a china service which probably belonged to Piero Ridolfi, who married a daughter of Lorenzo il

Lorenzo Lotto, Madonna del latte, *dating from c. 1525. Room 40.*

Magnifico. The splendid pieces date from 1515–1520 and were probably the work of a Venetian bottega.
They are decorated with *Stories of Orpheus* taken from Ovid's *Metamorphoses* and the *Hypnerotomachia Poliphili*. The other rooms on the second floor of the museum are now used for temporary exhibitions.

16th-century Graeco-Roman painter,
The Wedding at Cana,
Sala dei Madonneri Greci del XVI e XVII secolo. Room 41.

Orazio Fontana, Carafe decorated with an allegory of Strength, *ceramic. Room 42.*